This Book Belongs to:

______________________________________

# God’s Archangels
# The Story of Michael, Gabriel and Raphael



ISBN: 979-8-9953818-1-5



Published by Angel Light Publishing

## Why are they called Archangels?

Archangels are given this title because they have higher rank and special roles compared to other angels.

- **They are leaders among angels.**
  They guide or oversee other angels, much like captains or commanders.
- **They carry the most important messages from God.**
  While all angels are messengers, archangels are chosen for big, history-changing missions.
- **They have specific roles or responsibilities.**
  Each archangel is often associated with a purpose, such as:

Protection
Healing
Delivering messages
Spiritual battle against evil

"Archangels are God's special helpers—chosen to do the most important jobs and bring the biggest messages from heaven."

Archangels are special angels chosen by God for the most important missions. They are not gods—they are created beings, but they are very powerful servants of God.

The Catholic Church officially recognizes three archangels by name:

**Archangel Michael**
**Archangel Gabriel**
**Archangel Raphael**

These names come directly from Scripture.

**In the Bible:**

Archangels appear in both the Old and New Testaments:

Michael appears in the Book of Daniel and Revelation as a protector and warrior.

Gabriel appears in Daniel and in the Gospel of Luke as a messenger.

Raphael appears in the Book of Tobit as a healer and guide.

From the earliest days of Christianity, the Church recognized that these angels had special authority and closeness to God.

In the Catholic Church

The Church teaches that angels are part of a heavenly hierarchy (like a family with different roles). Archangels belong to one of the higher choirs, meaning they are entrusted with important responsibilities involving humanity.

The Church also celebrates them together on **September 29 (Feast of the Archangels).**

Long ago, before the world began,
God created angels—

shining spirits of light,

filled with love and goodness.

Some angels sang.

Some carried messages.

Some helped guide and protect people.

Among them were three very
special angels.

They are called Archangels—

God's strongest helpers.

Their names were

Michael, Gabriel,

and Raphael.

Each one had a special mission from God.

## The Story of Michael

The first is Michael,

the brave protector.

His name means,

"Who is like God?"

Archangel Michael is a strong and brave angel.

More than anything,

Michael loved God.

But one day, an angel thought he was more important than God and he decided to not follow God anymore.

The other angels went to follow him. They wanted to choose their own way.

Michael stood tall and said,
"Our God is the King of Heaven and Earth. God is good, and we will follow Him."
Michael loved God very much. He always wanted to do what was right and good.

Michael and the faithful angels
protected heaven from evil.

Because of his courage,
Michael became the leader
of God's heavenly army.

Today, many people remember
Michael when they feel afraid.

Archangel Michael reminds us:
Be brave.
Choose what is good. We pray to him
to ask for protection from evil.

## The Story of Gabriel

Archangel Gabriel is an angel

who carried messages from God.

When God had important news,

Gabriel was often the one sent to share it.

Gabriel's name means,

"God is my strength."

One day, God sent Gabriel

to a young woman named Mary.

Mary was kind, humble, and faithful.

Gabriel appeared gently and said, "Do not be afraid, Mary, for you have found favor with God" (Luke 1:30).

"Hail, full of grace, the Lord is with you!" (Luke 1:28).
"God has chosen you
for something wonderful."

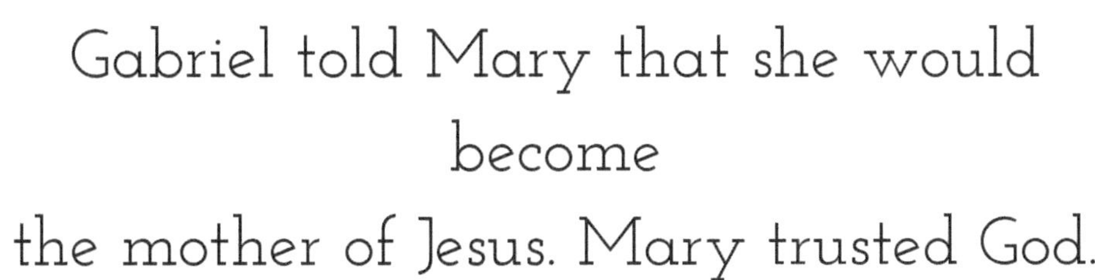

Gabriel told Mary that she would become
the mother of Jesus. Mary trusted God.

"I am the Lord's servant. May it be done to me as you have said."
Luke 1:38

Gabriel was chosen by God
to carry His holy message.
He reminds us that when we listen to
God
and speak with love,
we too can share His good news.

His visit to Mary, known as the
Annunciation, is a cornerstone of
Christian belief.

He is the Archangel known as God's messenger.
He spreads the Gospel of Jesus and the spirit of revival and the TRUTH about Jesus Christ.
So if you need clarity and assurance, you can ask for his help.

"Nothing is impossible with God"
(Luke 1:37)

# The Story of Raphael

Raphael is the Archangel

who guides and heals.

He helps people

on their journeys.

His name means "God heals" or "God's cure," identifying him as a divine healer and protector.

In the Bible, Raphael (disguised as a human named Azariah) helped a boy named Tobias.

Tobit sent his son Tobias to Media to recover a silver deposit. He was traveling far from home.

Raphael walked beside him
and kept him safe.

He helped Tobias
through many challenges.

At the end of the journey,
Raphael helped heal Tobias's father
who could not see.

"Blessed be God, and blessed be his great name" is spoken by Tobit in **Tobit 11:14**

Tobias learned
something amazing.

The kind guide beside him
who helped him on his journey and
the healing of his father was an
angel sent by God.

"Take courage! God's healing is near; so take courage" is a message of hope found in the Bible, specifically spoken by the archangel Raphael to a distressed, blind man named Tobit in the Book of Tobit (5:10).

Archangel Raphael reminds us
that God never leaves us alone.
He sends help, healing, and guidance
exactly when we need it most.

God sent three special archangels
to care for His people.
Michael stands strong to protect,
Gabriel brings joyful messages,
and Raphael walks beside us with
healing and care.
Through them, we are reminded
that God's love is always with us.

Archangel Michael
Archangel Gabriel
Archangel Raphael

# Bible Verses About the Archangels:

## Michael (Protector & Leader of Heaven's Army)

**Daniel 12:1**

"At that time there shall arise Michael, the great prince, guardian of your people..."

Michael is shown as a protector of God's people.

**Revelation 12:7-8**

"Then war broke out in heaven; Michael and his angels battled against the dragon..."

Michael leads God's angels in victory over evil.

**Jude 1:9**

"When the archangel Michael... disputed with the devil..."

Michael stands for God's authority and justice.

# Gabriel (Messenger of God's Good News)

Luke 1:26-28

"The angel Gabriel was sent from God... to a virgin named Mary...
"

Gabriel brings the greatest message—Jesus is coming.

Luke 1:19

"I am Gabriel, who stand before God..."

Gabriel is close to God and chosen to deliver His message.

Daniel 8:16

"Gabriel, help this man understand the vision."

Gabriel helps people understand God's plans.

**"Nothing is impossible with God" (Luke 1:37)**

# Raphael (Healer & Guide)

(Found in the Catholic Book of Tobit in the Bible)

Tobit 12:15

"I am Raphael, one of the seven angels who stand and serve before the Glory of the Lord."

Raphael reveals he is one of God's special angels.

Tobit 12:6

"Bless God, give him praise... for he has shown you great kindness."

Raphael teaches gratitude and faith.

Tobit 11:7-8

(Raphael guides Tobias to heal his father's blindness)

Raphael brings healing and guidance.

**"Take courage! God's healing is near; so take courage"**

Book of Tobit (5:10)

## Prayer to Saint Michael

**Written by Pope Leo XIII in 1884**

St. Michael the Archangel,
defend us in battle.
Be our protection
against the wickedness and snares of the devil.
May God rebuke him, we humbly pray,
and do thou, O Prince of the heavenly host,
by the power of God,
cast into hell Satan
and all the evil spirits
who prowl about the world
seeking the ruin of souls.
Amen.

## Prayer to Saint Gabriel

St. Gabriel the Archangel,
messenger of God's good news,
help us to listen to God's voice
and share His message with love.
Guide our words
so they bring hope, peace,
and joy to others.
Amen.

## Prayer to Saint Raphael

St. Raphael the Archangel,
healer and guide,
walk beside us on our journey.
Bring healing to our hearts and bodies,
and lead us safely
along God's path.
Amen.

## Short Prayer to All Three

Saint Michael, protect us.
Saint Gabriel, guide us.
Saint Raphael, heal us.
Holy angels, pray for us.
Amen.

God is with you always.

# Discover the Author's Other Books

**My Guardian Angel:**
**A Gift from God**
Guardian Angel Book
for Babies and Toddlers.

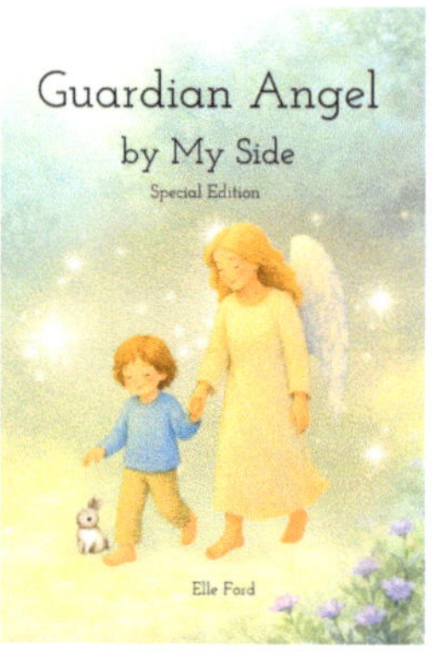


**Guardian Angel by My Side**
The Story of Love and Protection
Continues as the child grows.

**My Guardian Angel of Good Choices**
Angels guiding us to make the right choices. Show love, respect, compassion and other values.

**My Angel in the Sky**
For our Loved ones we lost and now our Angels guiding us. A story of healing, connection and love. The Hardcover version includes the book and a healing journal.

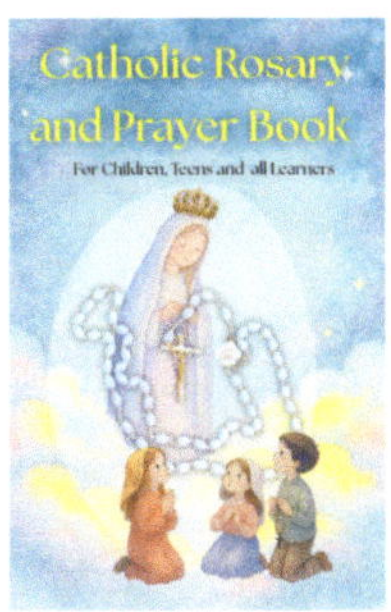


**Catholic Rosary and Prayer Book**

Teaching our kids Catholic prayers and early love for the Rosary.

**Euan and the Brave Backpack**

Helping our kids overcome first day of school jitters and big emotions.

Follow the Author page to discover more books and stay updated on new releases.

If you found this book meaningful, we would truly appreciate your review.

Thank you.

www.ingramcontent.com/pod-product-compliance
Lightning Source LLC
LaVergne TN
LVHW052301100826
845147LV00001B/113

* 9 7 9 8 9 9 5 3 8 1 8 1 5 *